Nineteen @ Nine

OrangeBooks Publication

Smriti Nagar, Bhilai, Chhattisgarh - 490020

Website: **www.orangebooks.in**

© **Copyright, 2021, Author**

All rights reserved. No part of this book may be reproduced, stored in a retrieval system, or transmitted, in any form by any means, electronic, mechanical, magnetic, optical, chemical, manual, photocopying, recording or otherwise, without the prior written consent of its writer.

First Edition, 2021

ISBN: 978-93-90837-78-6

Printed in India

Nineteen @ Nine

Aaliyah Jain

OrangeBooks Publication
www.orangebooks.in

For My Family

Foreword

At nine, one sees the real world—not through a glass, darkly. That is why when young Aaliyah captures magical moments in her poetry you are impressed by the authenticity of her world, her questions, her curiosity.

For me, this thin sheaf of her poems was like catching the last train back to innocence.

Pritish Nandy, *Poet, Journalist, Filmmaker, Former Member of Parliament.*

Index

- *A New Day* *1*
- *I Wonder* *3*
- *Squirrels* *5*
- *My Window My World* *7*
- *Rainbow In My Dream* *9*
- *Butterfly* *11*
- *Unicorns* *13*
- *Trees* *15*
- *Beautiful Birds* *17*
- *Beautiful Colours* *19*
- *Guess The Pet* *21*
- *Friends* *23*
- *Daughter's Day* *25*
- *My Family* *27*
- *Teachers* *29*
- *Father's Day* *31*
- *Playing Badminton* *33*
- *Mamma's Bakery* *35*
- *Gods* *37*

A New Day

The flowers are shining bright
The sky is blue and clear
The birds are singing melodiously
Pleasing to my ears

Everyone stays home
My father's office is at home
Very few people go outside
My school is now in the phone

Hope this virus soon leaves the Earth
And happiness takes new birth

I Wonder

How big is the Universe?
How many are the Stars?
How bright is the Sun?
Does anyone live on Mars?

How hot is Venus?
How big is the Moon?
How cold is Uranus?
I am curious to learn these things soon!

---- *Aaliyah Jain* ----

Squirrels

Everyday in the afternoon
I give peanuts to the squirrels
They are not like squirrels to me
They are like my angels

Some of them are big
And some of them are small
Their skin feels like fur
And their eyes look like balls

Whenever I give peanuts to them
They start squeaking at me
Sometimes they play with each other
Which makes me happy

---- Nineteen @ Nine ----

My Window My World

Whenever I get bored
I look out from my window
I see so many things
From the sunrise to the sunset glow

Sometimes I see families talking
Sometimes I see dogs sleeping
Sometimes I see birds flying
And sometimes I see squirrels eating

I hear new birds chirping
I see Aeroplanes take-off and land
I see gardeners planting trees
I see children playing in the sand

It's not just a window
It's like a whole world to me
Whatever I see from it
Makes me smile, makes me happy

Rainbow In My Dream

In my dream last night
I saw a colourful rainbow
It was shining very bright
Like a diamond with the glow

The rainbow was very beautiful
Last night in my dream
Rainbow's reflection appeared in the sea
As the water was very clean

Butterfly

Once I saw a butterfly
Red and pink and white
Dazzling in the sunshine
Moving left and right

Is it soft like butter?
Or is it soft like fur?
Wish I could play with it
And chit-chat with her!

---- *Aaliyah Jain* ----

Unicorns

Are unicorns imaginary creatures?
Or are the unicorns real?
Do they look like a horse?
Or they look like deer?

Why are they so colourful?
Why are they named unicorns?
Do they wear nothing?
Or they wear uniforms?

Are they rude?
Or they are kind?
These are the questions
That are in my mind

Trees

Trees are good for energy
Trees are good for health
Trees are good for our lives
Trees are the biggest wealth

Trees provide us oxygen
Trees provide us flowers
Trees provide us shade
And give us lots of power

Beautiful Birds

So many colourful birds
So many birds are there
Some of them are common
And some of them are so rare

How beautiful the birds are
How easily they fly in the air
I love the way they eat their food
I love how they take their baby's care

I wish I too could fly like them
And see the world upside down
Feel the wind on my face
And not tumble down!

---- *Aaliyah Jain* ----

Beautiful Colours

My favourite colour is blue
And my friends love it too
My mother's favourite is brown
And she has that colour's crown
Papa's favourite is green
And I think it's very clean
Grandma's favourite is pink
And it's very pretty I think
Grandpa's favourite is red
That's what he said!
All the colours are beautiful
And they make the world so cheerful!

---- Aaliyah Jain ----

Guess The Pet

In my neighbour's house
I saw a cute pet
It was white and grey
And it was very fat

It had soft legs
Can you still guess?
It makes the sound of meow
Now you know it's a cat

Friends

Sun is important for light
Eyes are important for sight
Water is important for thirst
Friends are important for life

Food gives us energy
Exercise gives us health
Family gives us love and care
Friends give us everlasting wealth

---- *Aaliyah Jain* ----

Daughter's Day

Today is Daughter's day
And I am feeling very special
My father made a card for me
Which had a dancing girl, oh so wonderful!

My grandparents gifted me some money
My mother started to cook and bake
She made a delicious pasta
And a very delicious cake

My Family

My family members love me so much
They always take care of me
They have always made me smile
Since I was a baby

They always fulfill my wishes
They play with me like my friends
I enjoy every moment
Together which we spend

Teachers

Learning with you
Is very fun
You give us light
Like the sun

You take care of us
Like our parents
You smile with us
Like our friends

Father's Day

My papa my hero
I love playing with you
My papa my precious treasure
You always give me pleasure

My papa my friend
I love the time which with you I spend
My papa my life
I love when you take me for a drive

Playing Badminton

I went downstairs with my father
First time after lockdown
We played for few minutes
In the lushy green playground

I hit the shuttle cock hard
And it went too high
And for a moment I thought
That it will touch the sky

Mamma's Bakery

My mother loves to cook food
And she also loves to bake
She makes cupcakes, pastries
And well decorated cakes

She makes cakes on occasions
For her friends and family
Some of them have little hearts
And some have flowers and trees

Gods

Where do Gods live?
How do they see everyone?
Why can't we see them?
Are they multiple or just one?

Can anyone see gods?
Do gods really live in heaven?
Why can't they talk to us?
Why can't we talk to them?

I thank the gods for
Everything they gave me
I hope they make everyone smile
And everyone remains happy

About Aaliyah

Aaliyah is a student of Class V, GD Goenka School, Dwarka, New Delhi. Nineteen @ Nine is Aaliyah's first book.

www.ingramcontent.com/pod-product-compliance
Lightning Source LLC
LaVergne TN
LVHW021240080526
838199LV00088B/5289